MAKING
MOVIES

Movie Makeup, Costumes, and Sets

by Geoffrey M. Horn

GARETH**STEVENS**
GS
P U B L I S H I N G
A Member of the WRC Media Family of Companies

Please visit our Web site at: www.garethstevens.com
For a free color catalog describing Gareth Stevens Publishing's
list of high-quality books and multimedia programs, call
1-800-542-2595 (USA) or 1-800-387-3178 (Canada).
Gareth Stevens Publishing's fax: (414) 332-3567.

Library of Congress Cataloging-in-Publication Data

Horn, Geoffrey M.
    Movie makeup, costumes, and sets / by Geoffrey M. Horn.
        p. cm. — (Making movies)
    Includes bibliographical references and index.
    ISBN-10: 0-8368-6838-2 — ISBN-13: 978-0-8368-6838-8 (lib. bdg.)
    1. Film makeup. 2. Costume. 3. Motion pictures-Setting and scenery.
I. Title. II. Series: Horn, Geoffrey M. Making movies.
PN1995.9.M25H67   2006
792.02'7—dc22   2006010312

This edition first published in 2007 by
Gareth Stevens Publishing
A Member of the WRC Media Family of Companies
330 West Olive Street, Suite 100
Milwaukee, WI 53212 USA

This edition copyright © 2007 by Gareth Stevens, Inc.

Concept: Sophia Olton-Weber
Managing Editor: Valerie J. Weber
Art direction and design: Tammy West
Picture research: Diane Laska-Swanke

Photo credits: Cover, MCA/Universal Pictures/Photofest; pp. 4, 8 © 20th Century
Fox Film Corp./Everett Collection; p. 5 © Patrick Riviere/Getty Images; p. 6 © Warner
Independent Pictures/courtesy Everett Collection; p. 7 Warner Independent
Pictures/Photofest; p. 10 © Robert Hepler/courtesy Everett Collection; p. 11 © Miramax
Films/courtesy Everett Collection; p. 12 © Sony Pictures Classics/courtesy Everett
Collection; pp. 13, 23, 24 © Everett Collection; p. 15 © Universal/Everett Collection;
p. 16 20th Century Fox/Photofest; pp. 17, 18 © Columbia Pictures/Everett Collection;
p. 19 © TriStar Pictures/Everett Collection; p. 21 Warner Brothers/Photofest; p. 22
Universal Studios/Photofest; p. 26 © Walt Disney/courtesy Everett Collection; p. 27
© Universal/courtesy Everett Collection; p. 29 © New Line/courtesy Everett Collection

Printed in the United States of America

1 2 3 4 5 6 7 8 9 10 09 08 07 06

Contents

Cover: You can hardly see Jim Carrey under all his makeup in this scene from *How the Grinch Stole Christmas*.

The "Look" of a Film

Every good film has its own "look." Many choices determine the look of a movie. Makeup, costumes, and settings are key. So are the types of cameras and lighting equipment used for the filming. Does the action take place in today's world or at some other time? Are the settings urban or rural? Indoors or outdoors? At night or during the day? Is the lighting soft or harsh? Will the colors be warm or cool? Answers to these questions — and many others — determine how a film will look.

Artistic Choices

In every film, the look needs to fit the story. For example, in *Planet of the Apes*, director Tim Burton shows a world where apes rule over

With clever costumes and makeup, a beautiful movie star like Helena Bonham Carter can look like an ape.

CELEBRITY SNAPSHOT
Catherine Martin

Born: January 26, 1965, in Sydney, New South Wales, Australia

Film Career: Production and costume designer

Academy Awards: Art direction and costume design on *Moulin Rouge* (2001)

Other Top Films: *Strictly Ballroom; Romeo + Juliet*

Backstory: Martin has designed sets but says her "first love really is clothes." She was in her teens when she decided to become a fashion designer. She has worked with director Baz Luhrmann on many projects. When she makes costumes, she's not just trying to make fancy clothes. The costumes must show something about each character.

Catherine Martin and Baz Luhrmann put the dazzle in *Moulin Rouge*.

The black-and-white look of *Good Night, and Good Luck* perfectly suits the film's 1950s setting.

humans. Rick Heinrichs designed the set for Ape City. Rick Baker created the makeup that made the actors' faces look like apes. Colleen Atwood helped design the ape costumes the actors wore.

In *Good Night, and Good Luck*, director George Clooney tells a very different story. *Good Night, and Good Luck* is a political drama based on true events. The hero is Edward R. Murrow, a TV newsman in the 1950s. The costumes are based on 1950s fashions. Makeup helps the actors look like the real-life characters they play.

Because TV programs back then were usually in black-and-white, Clooney gave the film a similar look. Cinematographer Robert Elswit used very bright indoor lighting. He says he aimed for "stark,

contrasty images that . . . feel rich with meaning." Murrow was a heavy smoker. (He died of lung cancer in 1965.) The lighting often highlights the smoke that swirls from his cigarettes.

A Musical Fantasy
Costumes, makeup, and sets take center stage in Baz Luhrmann's musical *Moulin Rouge*. The film takes place in a Paris club around 1900. The costumes and sets use bright, bold colors. The camera movements are dizzying. The filmmakers say they wanted to draw viewers into a fantasy world. They compare their film with *Alice in Wonderland* or *The Wizard of Oz*.

Behind the Scenes:
What Is Cinematography?

The person in charge of cameras and lighting is the director of photography, or DP. The DP is also called a cinematographer. *Cinematographer* comes from two words — *cinema* and *photographer*. Cinema is a fancy word for movies. Cinematography is the art of using a camera to make motion pictures.

The DP works with the director to create the right look for the film. Costumes, makeup, and sets all need to be shot the right way to look their best.

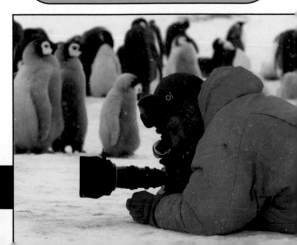

Cinematographers braved extreme cold to film *March of the Penguins*.

Behind the Scenes:
Matte Painting

Filmmakers have many ways to give each scene a special look. One common method is matte painting. A matte painting is a piece of art created for a particular scene. It is combined with a live-action shot to make something look real that isn't.

Suppose a script calls for a scene near an old temple. The film crew could try to find a real temple site. Or the crew could build a full-size model of a temple. But it's much cheaper just to have an artist paint a picture of a temple. The camera then shoots the matte painting along with the actors. That way, the temple becomes part of the scene.

The earliest matte paintings were on glass. Today, matte work is often done on a computer. Then the computer combines digital art with a live-action shot. The result is a single image.

Although the story is based in Paris, not a single second of the film was shot there. Everything was filmed indoors at Fox Studios in Australia. Matte paintings, sets, costumes, models, and visual effects create the look of Paris a century ago.

In *Moulin Rouge*, film artists used matte paintings and colorful effects to make a studio in Australia look like a fabulous Paris nightclub.

Costume Design

When you were younger, did you like to play dress-up? Did you enjoy wearing a costume and looking like a monster, a princess, or Spiderman? Now that you're older, you probably don't do it much anymore, except on Halloween. Actors are different. If they're lucky, they get to play dress-up 365 days a year.

All actors in movies wear costumes. In some films, the costumes may look like today's fashions. But each outfit is carefully chosen. Are the clothes casual or formal? Goofy or serious? Colorful or drab? Wrinkled or neat? Each choice tells us something about a character's values, wealth, and self-image.

Costume Dramas

A costume drama is a movie or play whose costumes and sets capture the look of a particular time and place. *The Ten Commandments* is a costume

9

CELEBRITY SNAPSHOT
Sandy Powell

Born: April 7, 1960, in London, Great Britain

Film Career: Costume designer

Academy Awards: *Shakespeare in Love* (1998); *The Aviator* (2004)

Other Top Films: *Velvet Goldmine; Gangs of New York*

Backstory: Powell has always loved clothes. When she was a little girl, she enjoyed dressing up. She also liked making costumes for her dolls. Her mother taught her to sew. As a designer, Powell has made costumes in many different styles. A big challenge is making clothes for a character who has bad taste in fashion. "Your natural instinct is to make people look fabulous," she says. "But most people don't."

Costume designer Sandy Powell holds her Oscar for *Shakespeare in Love*.

Powell's costumes in *Shakespeare in Love* are more than just fancy clothes. They show us the power and splendor of Queen Elizabeth and her court.

drama. It is based on events described in the Bible. One very famous costume is the robe worn by Moses, played by Charlton Heston. Five people designed the costumes for this 1956 film. The best known of the five was Edith Head. Between 1948 and 1977, she was nominated for thirty-five Oscars. She won eight. At the height of her career, she was as famous as any movie star.

Another good example of a costume drama is *House of Flying Daggers*. Its story takes place in China more than a thousand years ago. The costumes cost a lot to make — and look it. The clothes worn by Zhang Ziyi are especially beautiful. Emi Wada designed them.

11

Zhang Ziyi wore an outfit by Emi Wada for her drum dance in *House of Flying Daggers*.

In 2005, Zhang Ziyi starred in another costume drama, *Memoirs of a Geisha*. This story takes place in Japan during the first half of the twentieth century. Colleen Atwood won an Oscar for her costumes in the film. A year earlier, she did the costumes for the movie *Lemony Snicket's Series of Unfortunate Events*.

Fantasy Worlds

In fantasy and science-fiction films, costume designers don't need to worry about history. They can be as free as they want. What does Darth Vader look like? How do Imperial Storm Troopers dress? How hairy is Chewbacca? No one knew until John Mollo created the Oscar-winning costumes for the first *Star Wars*.

Adrian Greenberg made fancy gowns for some of the most glamorous women in Hollywood. But his best-known costumes are the ones he made for a fantasy film — *The Wizard of Oz*. Dorothy's ruby slippers? Greenberg made them, too.

A wicked witch wants what Dorothy is wearing — the magical ruby slippers.

Behind the Scenes:
So You Want to Be a Costume Designer . . . ?

Costume designers need many skills. They need to know how to make clothes. They need to draw well, so they can sketch their costume ideas. They must love movies, theater, and fashion.

Ask family members to teach you how to sew. Sharpen your design skills by making Halloween outfits for yourself and your friends. Practice making good-looking costumes from low-cost materials. Check out books on fashion history from your local library. Take art classes in school. Join a school drama group. Put together a portfolio of your best designs. You can show this portfolio when applying to college or looking for a job.

Many schools offer courses in clothing design. The Fashion Institute of Technology is a respected college in New York City. Parsons, also in New York, has a well-known design program. The Fashion Institute of Design and Merchandising has schools on the West Coast.

CHAPTER 3

Makeup

Movie makeup does many things. In films as in real life, face makeup can hide minor problems, such as mild acne and oily skin. The right makeup can make a male star look more handsome and a female star look more glamorous. Makeup can add years to a younger actor's face or smooth the wrinkles on an older actor. In war movies, makeup artists give the actors ugly-looking wounds and scars. In fight scenes, makeup often tells you who won and who lost.

Using Makeup to Tell a Story

In some films, makeup is at the heart of the action. *Nutty Professor II: The Klumps* is a good example. The movie opens in church. It's Professor Sherman Klump's wedding day. Mama and Papa Klump are there. Granny Klump, too. One actor — Eddie Murphy — plays all these Klumps and other people, too. The movie wouldn't work without Murphy's great comic talent.

CELEBRITY SNAPSHOT
Rick Baker

Born: December 8, 1950, in Binghamton, New York

Film Career: Makeup, special effects, producer

Academy Awards: Makeup for *An American Werewolf in London* (1981), *Harry and the Hendersons* (1987), *Ed Wood* (1994), *The Nutty Professor* (1996), *Men in Black* (1997), *Dr. Seuss' How the Grinch Stole Christmas* (2000)

Other Top Films: *Gorillas in the Mist; Batman Forever; Nutty Professor II: The Klumps; Planet of the Apes; The Ring*

Backstory: When he was growing up, Baker loved to watch horror films. He practiced using makeup by giving himself fake wounds. He thinks of himself as one of the luckiest guys in the world. "I do what I did as a hobby as a kid, you know, and make a living at it. I get paid to make toys and play with them."

Rick Baker's special makeup turned Eddie Murphy into the "Nutty Professor" and other oddball characters.

In *Mrs. Doubtfire*, Robin Williams plays a divorced dad. He dresses up like a woman to get a job as his ex-wife's housekeeper. As Mrs. Doubtfire, Williams wore padding to give him a womanly shape, special face makeup, and a wig. Greg Cannom designed the makeup. Ve Neill applied it. Hair stylist Yolanda Toussieng did the wig. Cannom, Neill, and Toussieng all won Oscars for their work on the 1993 hit.

For each day of filming as Mrs. Doubtfire, Williams had to sit in the makeup chair for three hours or more. First, his real hair was slicked back and hidden under a wig cap. Next, eight pieces of foam latex rubber were fit together on his face and neck. The latex was then painted. This paint layer served as a base for many other layers of makeup. The makeup gave Mrs. Doubtfire a "peaches and cream" look. Neill says she left some "splotchiness" around the cheeks and neck, "like an old lady would have."

The other great talent behind *Nutty Professor II* is Rick Baker. Baker is one of the best makeup artists in movies today. He won the very first annual Oscar for makeup with *An American Werewolf in London* (1981). As of 2006, he had won six Academy Awards, more than any other makeup artist.

To become Mrs. Doubtfire, Robin Williams wore a dress and padding on his body; a wig on his head; and latex, paint, and makeup on his face.

Baker won an Oscar for creating the weird creatures in *Men in Black*.

Baker uses many tools in his work. To turn Murphy into the different Klumps, he used prosthetic makeup. In this method, pieces of latex are glued to the actor's face. The latex is then painted to look more natural. Prosthetic makeup can completely change an actor's appearance.

Creatures with Features

Sci-fi and fantasy films let makeup artists do some of their most creative work. For example, Rick Baker made the alien creatures in *Men in Black*. This very funny 1997 movie stars Tommy Lee Jones and Will Smith as secret agents. Their job is

17

to protect the earth from aliens, "the scum of the universe."

Some aliens in *Men in Black* are real people with special costumes and face makeup. Others are purely digital. Still others, like the "worm guys," are puppets. Baker created the alien makeup. He also made some of the puppets. One puppet is the alien baby that Will Smith — as Agent J — helps to deliver.

It's a . . . what?! Will Smith holds an alien baby — a puppet, actually — in *Men in Black*.

Stan Winston is another great sci-fi makeup artist. He created the T-1000 robot in *Terminator 2: Judgment Day*. The T-1000 has a liquid-metal look. To create that look, actor Robert Patrick wore special makeup. The movie mixes live-action shots of Patrick with computer graphics. For his work on *Terminator 2*, Winston won Oscars for both makeup and visual effects. "We design characters," he says. "It's not about what are the special effects. . . . It's what are the special characters."

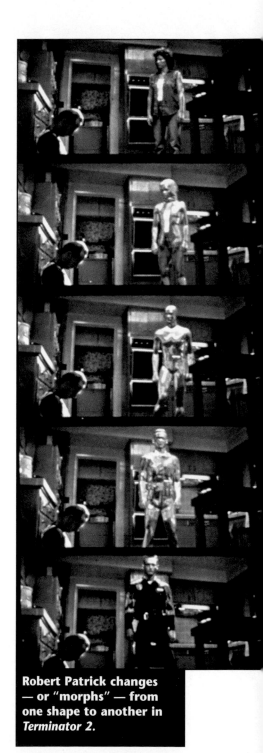

Robert Patrick changes — or "morphs" — from one shape to another in *Terminator 2*.

CHAPTER 4

Sets and Locations

Every scene in a movie takes place somewhere. In planning a film, the director must decide where each scene will be shot. Many scenes are filmed on a soundstage. In some ways, a soundstage is like a regular stage in a theater. The main difference is that a soundstage is set up especially for recording sound.

Each studio has one or more soundstages. The studio may also have a "back lot." The back lot is an open-air space where outdoor scenes can be filmed. In the early days of movies, almost every Western was shot on the back lot. Each back lot had a typical Western town that might be used in film after film.

Designing and Dressing Sets

Without sets, a soundstage or back lot is nothing but bare walls, lights, and equipment. Sets can make a soundstage look like just about anything.

CELEBRITY SNAPSHOT
Stuart Craig

Born: April 14, 1942

Film Career: Production designer

Academy Awards: *Gandhi* (1982), *Dangerous Liaisons* (1988), *The English Patient* (1996)

Other Top Films: *The Elephant Man; The Mission;* the *Harry Potter* series

Backstory: On the *Harry Potter* movies, Craig got a lot of help from author J. K. Rowling. She drew a map showing her vision of Hogwarts castle and everything around it. "She had a very, very exact and precise understanding of her world and her creation," says Craig. "She was able to give it to us, and that became our bible."

Stuart Craig designed this stunning view of Hogwarts at night.

Vince Vaughn and Jennifer Aniston share a so-not-together moment in *The Break-Up*. Even a simple living-room set involves dozens of choices.

Many people work on the sets for a major movie. Along with the director, the production designer decides how the physical world of the film will look. The person who actually designs the sets is called the set designer or art director. Carpenters build the sets. Scenic artists paint them. Finally, set dressers fill them with objects of various kinds.

Suppose you're shooting a scene on a soundstage. The scene takes place in a family living room. You need more than painted walls to make the room look real. You also need furniture and decorations. Chairs? A table? A sofa? Carpeting on the floor? Curtains on the windows? Paintings on the walls? You may need any or all of these things. Each item will say something about the people who live there.

Location Shooting

Scenes that are not filmed on a soundstage or back lot are shot "on location." Many directors think location shooting makes a film feel more real. For example, the film *Crash* takes place in Los Angeles. Many scenes in the movie were shot at various sites in L.A. Woody Allen likes to shoot many of his films at locations in New York City. So does director Martin Scorsese.

Behind the Scenes:
Images of the Future

Have you ever wondered what the world might look like in fifty or one hundred years? One of the first filmmakers to picture the future was Fritz Lang from Austria. His 1927 movie *Metropolis* showed rich people living in a city with very tall skyscrapers. Beneath the city are the workers, who live like slaves. Sets, models, and matte paintings show the upper and lower worlds. They offer a scary picture of the future.

Two more recent movies also show visions of the future. Stanley Kubrick finished *2001: A Space Odyssey* in 1968. His movie features a computer named HAL. When HAL goes crazy, it kills almost everyone around. Ridley Scott's *Blade Runner* dates from 1982. The production design imagines L.A. in 2019. How much of the filmmakers' vision has come true already? Check out the movie and judge for yourself.

Model makers for *Metropolis* built the city of the future — on a tabletop!

The 1959 film *North by Northwest* has a chase scene at Mount Rushmore. In the scene, actor Cary Grant hides among the huge carvings of U.S. presidents. At first, director Alfred Hitchcock wanted to shoot the film on location. "I wanted Cary Grant to hide in Lincoln's nostril and have a fit of sneezing," he said. The people who manage Mount Rushmore hated the idea. They asked Hitchcock how he would like it if they had Lincoln play the scene in Cary Grant's nose!

Hitchcock found a clever way to solve the problem. He had Robert Boyle build large models of the carvings back at the studio. The famous Mount Rushmore chase scene really took place in a Hollywood back lot.

Alfred Hitchcock wanted to shoot this scene on the real Mount Rushmore but had to use models instead.

All that hard work paid off. The three films earned more than $3 billion worldwide. They were nominated for a total of thirty Oscars. (They won seventeen.) The series opened new pathways for the movie industry. Weta showed filmmakers fresh ways to combine great costumes, makeup, sets, and effects to create a dazzling film fantasy.

The Return of the King — the final film in *The Lord of the Rings* series — won eleven Oscars for 2003, including best picture.

Glossary

back lot — in a movie studio, an open-air section that is used for filming outdoor scenes.

backstory — the background story to something seen on screen.

costume drama — a movie or play whose costumes and sets capture the look of a particular time and place.

digital — created by computer.

latex — a form of rubber or plastic.

matte painting — a painting that is combined with a live-action shot to give a particular look to a scene.

musical — a film or play with lots of singing and dancing.

nominated — named or suggested as a candidate for a particular honor or position.

portfolio — a collection of drawings or designs.

production designer — the person directly responsible for the physical world of the film.

prop — a movable object used in a scene.

prosthetic makeup — a way of making major changes in an actor's appearance by gluing pieces of latex to an actor's skin.

set — scenery built for use in a movie or play.

soundstage — in a movie studio, a stage that is set up for recording sound.

To Find Out More

Books

Eyewitness: Costume. Eyewitness Books (series).
L. Rowland-Warne (Knopf)

The Lord of the Rings: The Making of the Movie Trilogy.
Brian Sibley (Houghton Mifflin)

Makeup Artist. Careers Without College (series).
Kathryn A. Quinlan (Capstone Press)

Videos

House of Flying Daggers (Sony) PG-13

Men in Black (Sony) PG-13

Moulin Rouge (20th Century Fox) PG-13

2001: A Space Odyssey (Warner Home Video) G

Web Sites

Art Directors Guild
www.artdirectors.org
Includes awards pages and links to training programs

Costume Designers Guild
www.costumedesignersguild.com
Includes awards pages and costume designers' hall of fame

Weta Workshop
www.wetaworkshop.co.nz
The film company behind *The Lord of the Rings*

Publisher's note to educators and parents: Our editors have carefully reviewed these Web sites to ensure that they are suitable for children. Many Web sites change frequently, however, and we cannot guarantee that a site's future contents will continue to meet our high standards of quality and educational value. Be advised that children should be closely supervised whenever they access the Internet.

Index

About the Author

Geoffrey M. Horn has been a fan of music, movies, and sports for as long as he can remember. He has written more than three dozen books for young people and adults, along with hundreds of articles for encyclopedias and other works. He lives in southwestern Virginia, in the foothills of the Blue Ridge Mountains, with his wife, their collie, and four cats. He dedicates this book to the Grandin Theatre and to his Roanoke film-club companions.